JUL 2013

O9-BRZ-417

DISCARD

CPL discards materials that are outdated
and in poor condition in order to make
room for current in-demand materials,
underused materials are offered for
public sale

EDGE BOOKS™

The Kids' Guide to

MONSTER TRUCKS

BY MICHAEL O'HEARN

Consultant:

Ralph Moore, President

Edge-Motorsports

Capstone press®

Mankato, Minnesota

Edge Books are published by Capstone Press,
151 Good Counsel Drive, P.O. Box 669, Mankato, Minnesota 56002.
www.capstonepub.com

Copyright © 2010 by Capstone Press, a Capstone imprint.
All rights reserved.
No part of this publication may be reproduced in whole or in part,
or stored in a retrieval system, or transmitted in any form or by any means,
electronic, mechanical, photocopying, recording, or otherwise, without
written permission of the publisher.
For information regarding permission, write to Capstone Press,
151 Good Counsel Drive, P.O. Box 669, Dept. R, Mankato, Minnesota 56002.

Books published by Capstone Press are manufactured with paper
containing at least 10 percent post-consumer waste.

Library of Congress Cataloging-in-Publication Data
O'Hearn, Michael, 1972–
    The kids' guide to monster trucks / by Michael O'Hearn.
    p. cm. — (Edge books. Kids' guides)
    Includes bibliographical references and index.
    Summary: "Describes a wide variety of monster trucks, including history,
design, and competitions" — Provided by publisher.
    ISBN 978-1-4296-3371-0 (library binding)
    1. Monster trucks — Juvenile literature. I. Title. II. Series.
TL230.15.O34 2010
796.7 — dc22   2009010959

Editorial Credits
Gillia Olson, editor; Veronica Bianchini, designer; Wanda Winch, media researcher

Photo Credits
Art Life Images/©BIGFOOT 4x4, INC, 6, 7 (top), 14, 20 (bottom), 27 (bottom),
    28; ©Dave & Bev Huntoon, 9 (bottom), 11, 12, 13, 17, 20 (top), 22, 23, 24
    (both), 25 (bottom), 26, 27 (top); ©Rich Schaefer RSEP, INC, 8; ©USA-1, 7
    (bottom), 9 (top)
David Vogelsberg, 19 (top)
Shutterstock/Fawn Illes, cover (tire tread); Felix Miozniknov, 4–5, 14–15, 16;
    Kenneth Vincent Summers, 21; Mark Yuill, cover (tracks); Peter Albrektsen,
    cover (truck)
unlimitedcustoms.com/Frank Schettini, 25 (top, both), 29 (top)
U.S. Air Force photo/Master Sgt. Scott Reed, 19 (inset)
www.robosaurus.com, 29 (bottom)

**Capstone Press dedicates this book to the memory of George Eisenhart, Jr.,
who assisted us with the publication of this book by sharing his valuable monster
truck expertise.**

Printed in the United States of America in Stevens Point, Wisconsin.
022011   006074R

TABLE OF CONTENTS

WELCOME TO THE SHOW

Welcome monster truck fans! Are you ready for some bone-jarring, ear-numbing, car-crushing action? Then you've come to the right place. We've got all your favorite big block, supercharged, mega-wheel monster trucks.

This book has all the history, the heroes, and high-flying action you can handle. We'll see how they build them and how they break them. We'll explore the danger, the daring, and the downright wild. Let's bring on the mud and rumble. Let's bring on the thunder!

The original monster trucks were just regular pickups with giant wheels. Bob Chandler gets credit for the very first monster truck, Bigfoot, built in 1975. Chandler built the blue 1974 Ford F-250 to promote his truck shop.

Chandler drove the truck off-road for fun. He pushed the truck to its limit. This tough treatment often led to broken parts. Chandler replaced each broken part with bigger and stronger parts. After putting on 48-inch (122-centimeter) tires, he truly had a monster. Chandler earned the nickname "Bigfoot" for his bold driving. Eventually his truck took on the name.

Fun Fact:

There have been a total of 16 Bigfoot trucks. But there is no Bigfoot 13 because 13 is considered an unlucky number.

In 1981, Chandler drove Bigfoot over two junk cars in a Missouri field and had it videotaped. Truck fans shared copies of the tape, and Bigfoot became a legend. Chandler kept tinkering with his beast. Bigfoot got its 66-inch (168-centimeter) tires in 1982.

Another early monster truck was King Kong, later called Awesome Kong. Besides giant wheels, this Ford boasted a **diesel** engine. It was the king of tug-of-war competitions. During tug-of-war contests, two trucks were hooked together back to back with a chain. Then, the trucks tried to pull each other over a line on the ground.

diesel — a fuel that ignites using hot compressed air; traditional gasoline engines use a spark to ignite the fuel.

Everett Jasmer's Chevy USA-1 gave Bigfoot some competition and fueled the rivalry between the two U.S. automakers. In 1983, the two trucks raced over a drag strip of junk cars on the TV show, *That's Incredible*. Bigfoot won, but USA-1 put up a good fight.

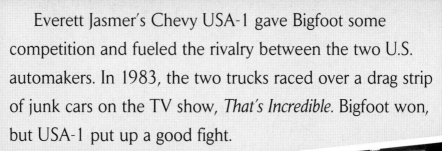

Bearfoot was a big Chevy Silverado. Bearfoot owner Fred Shafer liked big animals. That's how Bearfoot got its name. Fred kept two black bears that he sometimes brought along to early truck shows.

Big Trucks, Big Parts

Monster trucks require unique, heavy-duty parts. Some of the parts were designed for monster trucks, but many were originally made for other vehicles.

Monster trucks use a fiberglass "skin" rather than a metal body. Trucks also use decals instead of real headlights and tail lights. All of these items keep the truck's weight low for high-flying action.

Trucks may bounce up to 3 feet (.9 meter) between the truck's frame and the wheels. Shocks soften the force of the landing from the wheels to the truck. Most trucks use nitrogen gas shocks. They are similar to air shocks, but nitrogen is less affected by temperature than air.

axle — a rod in the center of a wheel around which the wheel turns

Most monster trucks have clear plastic floors. An airborne driver can look down and see where he's going to land.

Monster trucks weigh a minimum of 9,000 pounds (4,082 kilograms). This weight can break **axles** on hard landings. Monster trucks have used military, school bus, and forklift axles for their strength.

Monster trucks stand on 66-inch- (168-centimeter-) tall tires made for farm vehicles. The air pressure of the tires is about 10 pounds per square inch (psi). The average car tire takes about 32 psi. The low air pressure makes these tires soft, which makes for bouncy landings.

Monster trucks get their power from drag racing engines. These engines can crank out more than 1,500 horsepower. That's five times the horsepower of a regular pickup. The engine sits behind the driver's seat. Keeping the engine's weight toward the center of the truck helps improve the truck's balance.

MASTER MONSTER BUILDER

Dan Patrick has built 30 complete monster trucks and more than 70 chassis. He designed the first monster truck tube-frame chassis. Known as the "Patrick chassis," this design is common in modern monster trucks. His monster shop can fit six trucks at once.

horsepower – a unit for measuring an engine's power

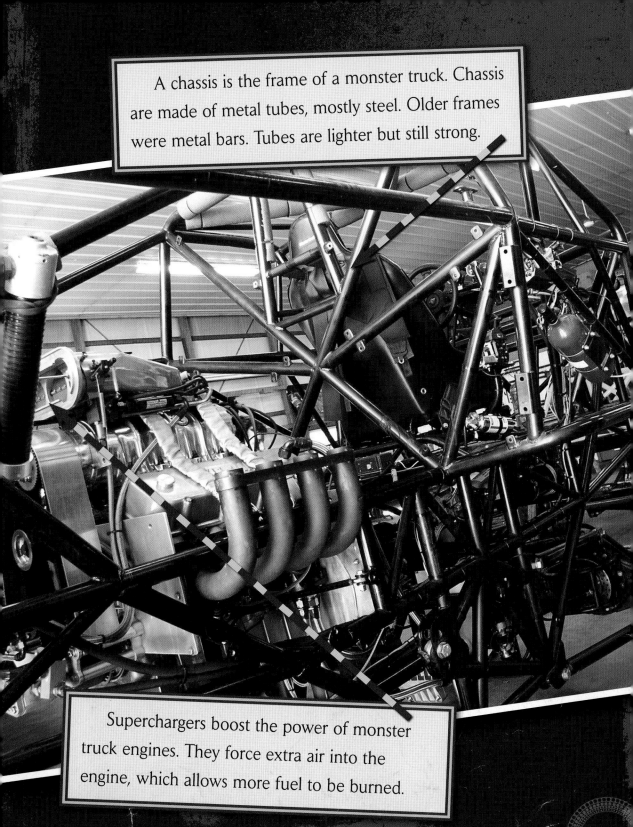

A chassis is the frame of a monster truck. Chassis are made of metal tubes, mostly steel. Older frames were metal bars. Tubes are lighter but still strong.

Superchargers boost the power of monster truck engines. They force extra air into the engine, which allows more fuel to be burned.

Monster Truck Safety

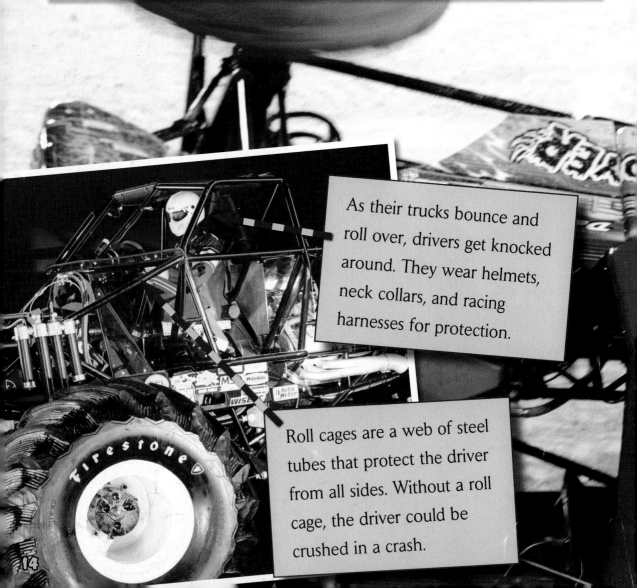

Monster trucks are heavy, powerful machines. And they crash a lot! The safety of drivers and fans requires special equipment.

As their trucks bounce and roll over, drivers get knocked around. They wear helmets, neck collars, and racing harnesses for protection.

Roll cages are a web of steel tubes that protect the driver from all sides. Without a roll cage, the driver could be crushed in a crash.

Fun Fact:

Every monster truck has a remote ignition interrupter (RII) that can shut down its engine. If a truck seems out of control, officials on the sidelines use the RII to keep fans and staff safe.

DRIVING A MONSTER TRUCK

"It feels pretty good 'til it lands." That's how Randy Brown, one of Grave Digger's drivers, described jumping in a monster truck. Although driving can be tough on their bodies, these drivers love their sport.

Breaking into the Business

The original monsters were made from stock trucks. Anyone could modify a truck and have a shot at competing. Today's monster trucks are custom vehicles. They cost about $150,000 to build, not including upkeep. Monster truck drivers need to be good enough to get sponsors.

Most drivers start as crew members on a monster truck racing team. They work as mechanics or drive the big rig that carries the truck to shows. In addition, they usually have experience with other kinds of racing.

Getting Licensed

Drivers must have a Monster Truck Racing Association (MTRA) certification. First, they get a Class B MTRA license, which allows them to learn the ropes. To get the Class A license, a driver must compete in 10 official MTRA races.

TRICK OF THE TRADE

Going airborne off a jump, you might think a driver would take his foot off the gas. Not the case. Drivers keep the tires spinning. Then the truck lands moving forward instead of crashing like a rock.

RACING AND FREESTYLING

All monster trucks are powerful, but which is the best? Promoters and drivers have found many ways to decide. Trucks compete at events like Monster Jam, Monster Nationals, and Monster Madness.

Monster trucks race two at a time. The trucks race side by side, either on straight or J-shaped tracks. They crush cars, fly off jumps, and run up steep hills.

Each monster truck event has up to 16 trucks competing. The winner of each race takes on the winner from another race, and so on. Finally, one truck beats all the others.

Some races are part of a points series. Drivers earn points for each race they win and for the fastest time in the whole event. At the end of the series, the driver with the most points wins the competition.

Fun Fact:

At most events, there's a pit party before the racing starts. People can meet the drivers and get an up-close view of their favorite trucks.

In freestyling, monster truckers try to wow the crowd. They do any kind of trick they can pull off. Drivers in freestyle events are often awarded points by judges. But in some competitions, the winner is chosen by the loudest audience applause.

One freestyle trick is a doughnut. The trucks spin in a circle, making a doughnut-shaped track in the dirt.

Fun Fact:

The longest jump ever was 202 feet (61.6 meters) over a 727 airplane. Dan Runte driving Bigfoot 14 pulled it off.

A skilled driver can bounce the truck onto its rear tires and keep driving. Monster wheelies are a major part of freestyle events. Sky wheelies are when the truck's wheels are at a 90-degree angle to the ground. Slap wheelies are when the driver goes into a wheelie off a bounce from a landing.

Monster truck designers are nothing if not creative. They've built many crazy and unique trucks, including these standouts.

The Black Stallion has been around since the early monster truck days. Mike Vaters added 40-inch (102-centimeter) tires to his street-driven Ford. Today, Stallion runs on 66-inch (168-centimeter) tires. Vaters is a seven-time Thunder Nationals champion.

The original Grave Digger was built from a 1951 Ford pickup chassis. It had a Chevy engine and lots of spare parts. In 1986, the truck received its graveyard paint job. Former owner and current driver Dennis Anderson is known for wild driving and super stunts. Grave Digger is one of the most popular monster trucks of all time.

The Raminator is — you guessed it — a Dodge Ram pickup truck. And with more than 2,000 horsepower, it's fast! Raminator has won six Performance Series racing titles.

The Batman truck looks like it came right out of Gotham City. It's the Batmobile on monster truck tires. Batman is a two-time Monster Jam racing champion.

Big Dummy 3 is more than a truck. With a monster stereo and a bed full of speakers, it's a party on wheels. The frame of the truck lifts 10 feet (3 meters) above the tires.

Dungeon of Doom was one of the scariest trucks out there. Its body was shaped like a skull with a rib cage over the box. Underneath the skin, the truck was originally Bigfoot 8.

Bigfoot 5 is so big it can drive over other monster trucks. Its tires are 10 feet (3 meters) tall, and 4 feet (1.2 meters) wide. They came off a military vehicle called the "Snow Train" that carried supplies across deep snow.

During the 1990s, monster trucks teamed up with professional wrestling to promote famous wrestlers. Hulk Hogan, Sting, Goldberg and The Undertaker all had wrestle trucks. Hulk Hogan's "Hulkster" truck had muscled arms reaching out from the cab.

The powder blue Ms. Bigfoot was no powder puff. This monster had a 1,000 horsepower engine. The first female monster truck driver, Marilyn Chandler, wife of Bob Chandler, made it fly.

OTHER MONSTER CREATIONS

Some machines in the monster truck world aren't trucks at all. Monster truck creators are limited only by their imaginations.

How do you get more monster than a monster truck? You build a monster tank. Popular in the late 1980s, monster tanks included Heavy Metal, Nitecrawler, and Bigfoot Fastrax. At 20,000 pounds (9,000 kilograms), they were twice the weight of a monster truck.

Monster Jerky is a unique monster. Its designer, Frank Schettini, was a dirt bike racer. He made a monster truck that was part dirt bike. To drive, Frank stands in a harness. He steers with handlebars and controls speed and braking with hand controls. It's hard for other drivers to control, but for Frank it comes naturally.

ROBOSAURUS

Robosaurus eats monster trucks for breakfast. This giant 40-foot- (12-meter-) tall robot has 12-inch (30-centimeter) teeth. Robosaurus breathes fire, too. A driver strapped inside the head controls the beast.

GLOSSARY

axle (AK-suhl) — a rod attached to the middle of a wheel on a vehicle; axles turn the wheels.

chassis (CHA-see) — the frame on which the body of a vehicle is built; the chassis holds together all the other parts of the truck.

diesel (DEE-zuhl) — a heavy fuel that ignites using hot compressed air; traditional gasoline engines use a spark to ignite the fuel.

fiberglass (FY-buhr-glas) — a strong, lightweight material made from woven threads of glass

harness (HAR-nuhss) — a seatbelt that straps over both shoulders for extra hold and safety

horsepower (HORSS-pow-ur) — a unit for measuring an engine's power

promote (pruh-MOTE) — to make people aware of something or someone; promoters are people who plan and raise awareness for events.

READ MORE

Levete, Sarah. *Monster Trucks.* Mean Machines. Chicago: Raintree, 2005.

Maurer, Tracy. *Monster Trucks.* Roaring Rides. Vero Beach, Fla.: Rourke, 2004.

Spalding, Leeanne Trimble. *Monster Truck Racing.* The Thrill of Racing. Vero Beach, Fla.: Rourke, 2009.

Young, Jeff C. *Trucks: The Ins and Outs of Monster Trucks, Semis, Pickups, and Other Trucks.* RPM. Mankato, Minn.: Capstone Press, 2010.

INTERNET SITES

FactHound offers a safe, fun way to find Internet sites related to this book. All of the sites on FactHound have been researched by our staff.

Here's all you do:

Visit *www.facthound.com*

FactHound will fetch the best sites for you!

INDEX